What are....?

DESERTS

Andy Owen
and
Miranda Ashwell

Heinemann
LIBRARY

First published in Great Britain by Heinemann Library
Halley Court, Jordan Hill, Oxford OX2 8EJ
a division of Reed Educational and Professional Publishing Ltd.
Heinemann is a registered trademark of Reed Educational and Professional Publishing Ltd.

OXFORD FLORENCE PRAGUE MADRID ATHENS
MELBOURNE AUCKLAND KUALA LUMPUR SINGAPORE TOKYO
IBADAN NAIROBI KAMPALA JOHANNESBURG GABORONE
PORTSMOUTH NH (USA) CHICAGO MEXICO CITY SAO PAULO

Designed by Susan Clarke
Illustrations by Oxford Illustrators (maps pp.23, 25, 27)
Printed in Hong Kong

02 01 00 99 98
10 9 8 7 6 5 4 3 2 1

ISBN 0 431 02359 X

British Library Cataloguing in Publication Data

Owen, Andy
   What are deserts?. – (Heinemann first library)
   1.Deserts – Juvenile literature
   I.Title II.Ashwell, Miranda III.Deserts
   551.4'15

Acknowledgements
The Publishers would like to thank the following for permission to reproduce photographs:
Barnaby's Picture Library, p.21; Bill Bachman, pp.22, 24, 26; Bruce Coleman Ltd, p.13 (Gerald
Cubitt), p.7 (Mr Jules Cowan), p.14 (David Hughes), p.9 (John Murray); FLPA, p.5
(W. Wisniewski), p.10 (Martin Withers); Magnum/Steve McCurry, p.19; Oxford Scientific
Films, p.11 (Marty Cordano), p.4 (Stan Osolinski); Planet Earth, p.29, pp.16, 18 (Thomas
Dressler), p.6 (John Evans), p.12 (Peter Stephenson), p.17 (Ronald Rogott); Tony Stone, p.15
(Frank Heroldt), p.28 (Duncan Wherrett)

Cover photograph: Oxford Scientific Films/Stan Osolinski

Our thanks to Betty Root for her comments in the preparation of this book.

Every effort has been made to contact copyright holders of any material reproduced in this
book. Any omissions will be rectified in subsequent printings if notice is given to the Publisher.

Contents

Some words are shown in bold, **like this**.
You can find out what they mean by looking
in the Glossary.

Deserts are dry

All deserts are dry places. It may not rain for months or years.

This desert is sandy

This desert is rocky

Most deserts are rocky or stony places.
Only special plants and animals can live
where it is so dry.

Flat and hilly deserts

Some deserts are flat so you can see a very long way. Crossing deserts can be difficult because there are few roads.

The Sahara Desert in Africa takes days to cross

These desert mountains have flat tops

Many deserts have hills and mountains.
The wind carries sand which cuts the
rocks into odd shapes.

Hot and cold deserts

Some deserts get very hot

The fierce heat plays tricks with the light. The hot ground can look like water but the water is not real. It is a **mirage**.

The Atacama Desert is
one of the coldest deserts

Not all deserts are hot. The Atacama Desert
in South America is cold because it is high up
in the mountains.

Days and nights

The desert sky often has no clouds. Without clouds in the way the sun makes the ground very hot. Animals must hide from the great heat.

In a desert there are few places to hide from the sun

Many animals sleep in the hot day and are awake at night

Deserts become cold at night. There are no clouds to keep in the warmth of the day. Many animals are busy in the cool night.

Rain in the desert

In some deserts it only rains for a few hours each year. This is enough for some special plants to grow.

A cactus plant holds water to use when it is dry

One of the driest places in the
world is the Namib desert in Africa

It may not rain in the driest deserts
for many years. This makes it hard
for anything to live there.

Desert storms

Strong winds whip the desert sand into the air. These **dust storms** can last for days. Smaller winds make swirling **dust devils** that last for a few minutes.

This is a dust devil

These dark clouds show that heavy rain is about to fall

Rain in the desert comes in heavy storms. They **flood** the land. Heavy rain washes away the sand.

Rivers in the desert

For most of the year this river is dry. It needs the rain to fill it with water. Without water you can see the bottom. This is called the **river bed**.

A dry river in the desert

When it rains the river quickly fills with water. It only rains for a short time so the river will only flow for a few hours. Soon the river will be dry again.

Water washes away the desert sand

The moving desert

The tops of sand **dunes** are called crests. The wind carries sand over the crest and drops it on the other side.

The desert wind blows the sand into beautiful shapes called dunes

The sand has been blown into this home

The wind spreads the desert sand. Sand
is blown across roads and into buildings.

Water in the desert

Without water people cannot live in
the desert. Water can be found in a
few special places. People walk for
days from one water hole to the next.

People come to this place in
the desert for water

People in this desert city use water in their homes and gardens. The water comes from under the ground. Water is also brought from a river many miles away.

Phoenix, in America, is a big city in the desert

Desert map 1

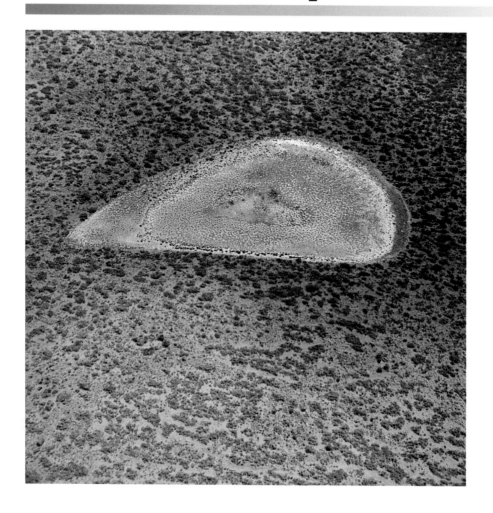

This photo shows part of a sandy desert in Australia. The pear shape is where water has been dried up by the hot sun. You can see salt that has been left behind after the water has gone.

Key

□ sandy desert

□ salty water

This map uses colours to show the same place as the photo. The orange colour shows the sandy desert. The grey colour tells us that any water here will be salty. On a map fresh water is shown as a blue colour.

Desert map 2

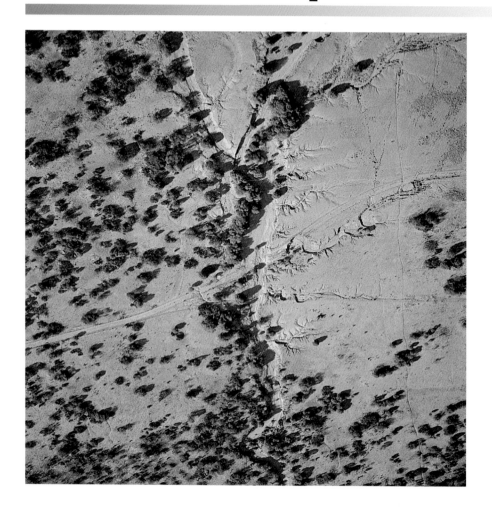

This photo is of a dirt road which crosses the desert in Australia. The road crosses a river. There is no bridge because the river is dry for most of the year.

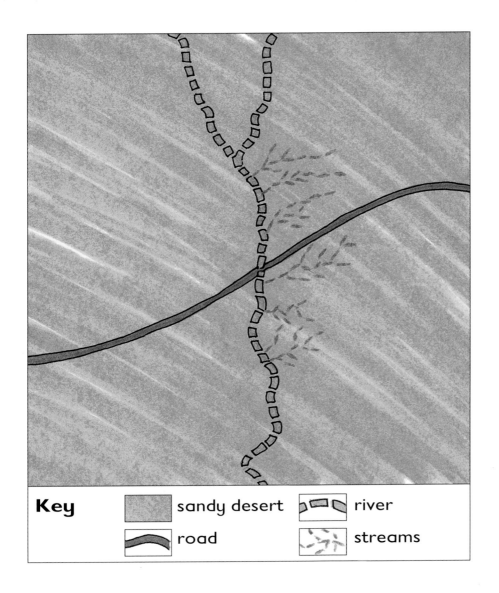

Key

	sandy desert		river
	road		streams

Rivers are shown on maps with a blue line. This river is shown with a broken blue line. This tells us that the river is dry for most of the year. You can also see some small streams which join the larger river.

Desert map 3

A huge rock from space landed in the desert a long time ago. It made a big hole called a **crater**. A road has been built so that people can come to see the crater.

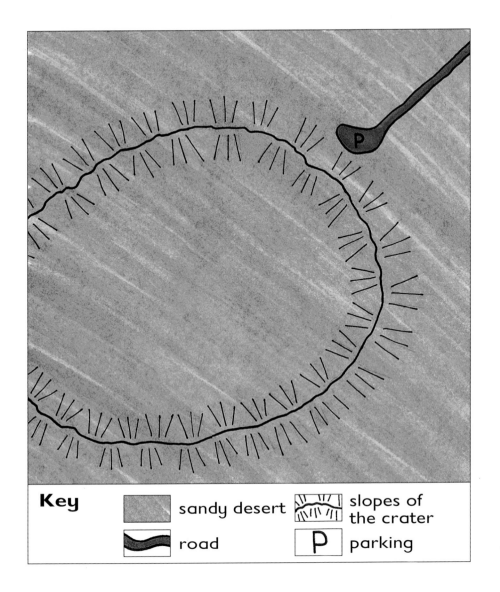

Key

▨ sandy desert	〰 slopes of the crater
～ road	P parking

People park their cars at the end of the road. They climb up the steep crater slopes and then down into the middle. The map shows these slopes with thin black lines.

Amazing desert facts

The Sahara Desert in Africa is the biggest desert in the world. This desert is nearly as big as the United States of America.

The biggest dunes in the world are in the Namib desert in Africa. Sand blown by the wind can strip the paint off a car.

Glossary

crater   a large hole formed by an explosion

dunes   hills made out of sand

dust devils   short storms that pick up sand

dust storms   when strong winds whip the desert sand into the air. This can last for several days

flood   water from a river that spills onto the land

mirage   when the hot air plays tricks with the light. For example, roads and sand can look as if they are covered in water

river bed   the bottom of a river

More books to read

Nicola Baxter. *Our Wonderful Earth.*
Two-Can, 1997

Claire Llewellyn. *Why do we have?*
Deserts and Rainforests.
Heinemann, 1997

Joy Palmer. *First Starts: Deserts.*
Franklin Watts, 1996

You may need help to read this book on deserts.

Neil Morris. *The World's Top Ten Deserts.*
Belitha Press, 1996

Index